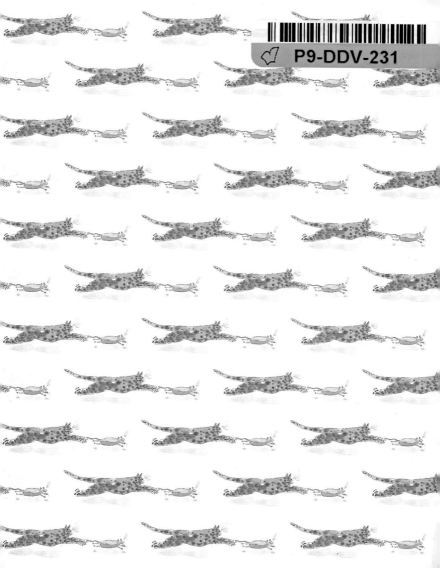

P9-DDV-231

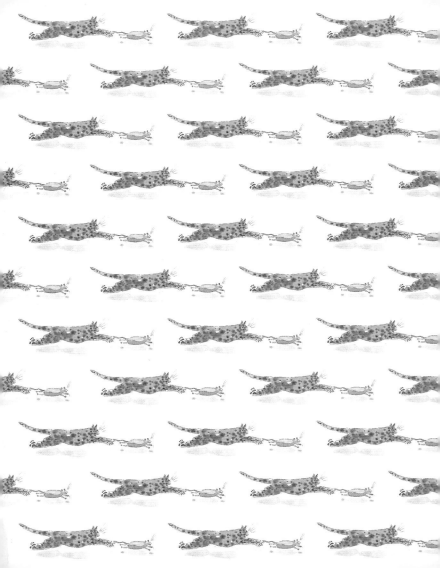

FENG SHUI FOR CATS

By Cats, For Cats

EDITED BY

RONI JAY

Sterling Publishing Co., Inc
New York

Published in 1998 by Sterling Publishing Company, Inc
387 Park Avenue South, New York, N.Y. 10016

10 9 8 7 6 5 4 3

Originally published in Great Britain in 1997 by Godsfield Press,
Laurel House, Station Approach, New Alresford,
Hampshire, SO24 9JH, U.K.

Distributed in Canada by Sterling Publishing
c/o Canadian Manda Group, One Atlantic Avenue, Suite 105
Toronto, Ontario, Canada M6K 3E7
Distributed in Australia by Capricorn Link (Australia) Pty Ltd.
P.O. Box 6651, Baulkham Hills, Business Centre
NSW 2153, Australia

Printed and bound in Hong Kong

Sterling ISBN 0-8069-7058-8

CONTENTS

風水

INTRODUCTION

There are plenty of books about feng shui for humans, but they won't tell you what you need to know. This book, however, is written by cats, for cats. The first thing you will want to know is: what is feng shui? Feng shui is an ancient Chinese art that is based on the principle that the world is full of stuff called ch'i. Ch'i is energy or life force; you can't see it, although more experienced cats can learn to smell it.

GOOD AND BAD FENG SHUI

Ch'i should always be on the move. If it is stopped it stagnates, and if it is funneled it flows too fast. If either of these things happens in your territory, it's bad news for you because it causes bad luck. Feng shui is all about making sure that the ch'i flows happily through your territory. Bad feng shui can lead to misfortunes such as infrequent feeding, lack of respect from humans, and the like. Good feng shui, on the other paw, can generate a safe comfortable territory with plentiful food supplies. It can even get the central heating turned up a few notches.

This book explains how you can assess the feng shui of your territory, and what to do if any areas need adapting to help the ch'i flow more smoothly. Sometimes a small change can make a big difference; sometimes you will need to make bigger changes, such as altering the places where you spray to mark your territorial boundaries, or even arranging for furniture to be moved around.

GETTING HUMAN COOPERATION

Creating good feng shui is an especial challenge for cats, since it can be difficult to elicit cooperation from your humans. Their agenda is not necessarily the same as yours. However, by following the advice in *Feng Shui for Cats* you will be able to create a harmonious territory full of warmth, comfort, and good food.

THE PRINCIPLES
OF FENG SHUI

The words "feng shui" are Chinese for "wind and water." Don't be alarmed by this – you aren't expected to get involved with wind to do feng shui, and you certainly won't need to get wet. The point is that ch'i flows through and around your territory all the time in the same way that air and water flow. It even flows round your food bowl. In extreme cases it can pour in a torrent or it can stagnate completely; both of these are unhealthy (especially if they happen near your food).

VARIOUS ASPECTS OF YOUR LIFE

The way ch'i flows in different parts of your territory affects different aspects of your life. In one area, for example, the feng shui will affect what the Chinese call your wealth; in other words your stockpile of cans of food, the number of comfortable cushions you have access to, the number of "pick your own" meals available in your territory – even the size and juiciness of the mice and other livestock involved.

WORKING OUT DIRECTIONS

Ch'i can flow from different directions, and the compass directions are very important in feng shui. This means you will need to know which way you are facing in different sections of your territory. Humans seem to have great difficulty establishing this, and have even developed compasses to help them. We have a far simpler method, that we will recap just in case you are too young to know it yet (or too sleepy to remember it).

You like to sleep in the sun. The sun rises in the east. So the place you sleep in every morning faces east. The reverse applies in the afternoons, when you will doubtless sleep somewhere that faces west. You can work out the remaining directions from this. Why humans can't come up with a simple technique like this is a mystery.

WHICH WAY DOES
YOUR TERRITORY FACE?

One of the first things you need to know to assess the feng shui of your territory is which way it faces. This determines which aspect of your life is influenced by each part of your territory.

TERRITORIAL RITES

The direction your territory faces is said by the Chinese to be determined by the direction that you normally enter it from. This is clearly ridiculous, since your territory is defined by the fact that it is a space that you never go beyond. And if you never leave it, how can you possibly enter it from any direction?

A different definition is clearly needed for cats and, fortunately, there is a way you can determine the direction of your territory. While the territory as a whole faces in no particular direction, the house or apartment you live in

[8]

does. It faces the way you normally leave and enter it. This may be through a cat flap; on the other paw you may not have a cat flap. Or you may have one, but prefer not to use it. Perhaps you come in through a window, or maybe you have trained your human to open the door for you.

YOUR FAVORITE ENTRANCE

Whichever entrance you use most is the important one. If you use more than one entrance, treat your favorite as the most important one – perhaps the one nearest the food bowl.

If you are one of those unfortunate cats who is kept cooped up and never allowed out, there is only one useful piece of advice. Escape and never come back. Find a new territory. If you can't flow smoothly in and out, neither can the ch'i, and the feng shui of your territory will be irredeemably awful.

THE PAH KWA

Now we get on to the really crucial bit. The pah kwa is a kind of plan you have to draw up (you can do it in your head if you haven't yet mastered the skill of holding a pen). It is divided into eight areas, and when you put it on top of a plan of your territory it tells you which part of the territory relates to which aspect of your life.

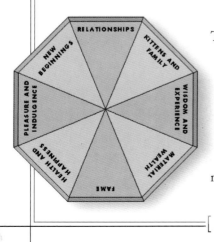

THE EIGHT AREAS

The eight areas of the pah kwa relate to fame and fortune, health and happiness, pleasure and indulgence, new beginnings, relationships, kittens and family, wisdom and experience, and material wealth.

風水

Place the middle of the pah kwa on the middle of your territory, with the fame section facing whichever way your territory faces. If your territory is square, round, or octagonal, each part of it will be covered by a section of the pah kwa, telling you which area of your life that section of territory affects.

MISSING SECTIONS

But what if your territory isn't a regular shape? And of course, it probably isn't. It may protrude in one direction to reach that shed where all the rats live, or it might miss out a chunk to fit round a large neighboring tomcat's territory without drawing attention to itself. This could

mean that you have no territory at all to accompany one or more sections of the pah kwa. A missing section of territory means that the related area of your life is missing. For example, cats who are locked outside at night usually find the pleasure area of their territory is missing.

ENLARGED SECTIONS

On the other paw, an enlarged section of territory suggests an abundance of whatever aspect of your life it relates to. In the area of relationships, for example, it probably means you live with a large family whom you have under control.

風水

As far as possible, use each section of your territory for the activities it relates to. So sleep in a suitable area such as pleasure and indulgence. If you were to sleep in, say, the relationships area, you would find that your relationships with humans and other cats would drift apart. Or, if your litter tray is in the wealth area, every time you bury your litter, you bury your wealth. Better to have it in your area of human relationships, as a constant reminder of how humans should be treated to keep them in their place.

MAKING CHANGES

Go round your territory and examine what you use each section of it for. Now see if this fits in with the pah kwa area that it falls in. If not, you will need to change (sorry, not a pleasant word for a cat, but some change is necessary to perfect the feng shui around you), and shift certain activities to more suitable locations. The good news is that once the changes are made, they're for keeps.

THE EIGHT AREAS
OF THE PAH KWA

et's have a closer look at the areas that your territory falls in to. You can tell whether the feng shui of these areas is good or bad by the quality of this aspect of your life. The following list gives you a general idea of the things that will be affected by the feng shui of each of these sections of your territory.

FAME AND FORTUNE

Is your territory too small? Are you under threat from neighboring cats or – worse – dogs? If so, look to this area to find the solution. If things are really bad, you may even be missing a chunk out of your territory here.

MATERIAL WEALTH

If you suffer from underfeeding, lack of warmth or other basic necessities, it is likely that there are problems in this section.

WISDOM AND EXPERIENCE

Not normally a problem for cats, but should you find that your judgment is less than perfect, or that your memory has momentary lapses, you should study this area closely.

KITTENS AND FAMILY

This area is often missing for cats that have been n**tered. For male cats that have not been abused in this way it may well be the largest section of territory. Female cats who do not enjoy motherhood should avoid this area (especially if it is close to any tomcats' territories), but those who enjoy it, on the other paw, should maximize the flow of ch'i and hang out here a lot, especially when in season.

RELATIONSHIPS

The most important relationship to consider here is with your human(s). Things can go sadly wrong with this relationship, especially if your human is short-tempered, or becomes preoccupied with minor considerations that draw their attention away from your needs. In these instances, this is the area where you will need to apply some of the remedies that we will be looking at later.

NEW BEGINNINGS

These mean change and a shift in routine, and are therefore best avoided by cats. Keep away from this part of your territory as much as possible, and break all the tenets of feng shui here by encouraging the ch'i energy to

風水

stagnate. Note: If this is the area where your food is provided, you will have to find other ways to change your feeding place.

PLEASURE AND INDULGENCE

This area cannot be too large. If necessary, fight to keep this part of your territory out of the grasp of other cats. Also make sure that, if this area falls inside the house, you have 24-hour access to all the rooms there.

HEALTH AND HAPPINESS

If you feel unsettled or discontented, this area probably contains the problem. Equally, if your human develops a tendency to drag you off to the v** for no apparent reason, turn your attention to this part of your territory. Look for places of stagnating ch'i and remedy them according to the solutions listed later on in this book.

NO ENTRY

PUSSY

THE FOUR ANIMALS

The Chinese will tell you about the four great animals that live at each of the main compass points. They influence the type of ch'i that flows from their direction. So the part of your territory that faces south, for instance, will get its ch'i from that direction, which is the home of the Red Phoenix. The personality of the four animals affects the energy that comes from each of their directions, so let's see what they are.

SOUTH — THE RED PHOENIX

This is the only animal that has more lives than we do. Not content with nine lives, the phoenix dies and is reborn on a neverending cycle. It burns to death, then rises alive from its own ashes. We do not suggest you try this yourself.

The phoenix is associated with expansiveness, light, joy, happiness, and other cheerful things, that means that you want to encourage ch'i from the south. One word of warning, though: the phoenix is not conducive to sleep, so don't overdo it.

NORTH — THE BLACK TORTOISE

Here's the sleepy animal for you. The tortoise is all about winter, mystery, sleep, somberness, and so on. If you encourage ch'i from the north, it will bring this very nurturing animal with it, so you could do worse than keep your kittens in a part of your territory open to ch'i from the north.

You will have realized that if you are indoors, the north side of the territory doesn't afford the sunniest sleeping spots. So you will need to look around for a room that faces the sun but lets in energy through doors and windows to the north.

WEST — THE WHITE TIGER

This animal is associated with strength, anger, bursts of energy, and even violence. It is thought by humans to be dangerous and unpredictable, but you will be able to live alongside it far more easily than they can, since the tiger is a cousin of ours and you will have a natural empathy with it.

The white tiger will lend you its strength and unpredictability for such activities as hunting and defending your territory, so try to arrange these activities in the west.

If you are attacked by a neighboring cat from a different direction, use your initiative to lure it round to the west, where you have a greater chance of seeing it off. (Do not leave this book lying around, on the other paw, or the neighboring cats will be trying to entice you into the west of their territories.)

EAST – THE GREEN DRAGON

The dragon is a creature of luck, kindness, wisdom, culture, and hope. The ch'i that flows from its direction is ideal for helping you think. You can do this in the mornings in a patch of sunlight from the east. (You may find it helps to close your eyes – just to help you concentrate, of course.)

The ch'i flowing from the east will give you the inspiration you need to find ways of "persuading" your humans to cooperate with you in improving the feng shui of your surroundings.

So those are the four animals. For each activity (or inactivity), encourage ch'i to flow from the direction of the animal that is conducive to it.

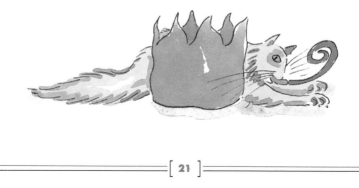

IDENTIFYING
BAD FENG SHUI

We've looked at directions and animals and the pah kwa, and we've seen what ch'i is, but we haven't said how you can tell if the flow of ch'i in a particular area is good or bad. You must be twitching your tail with impatience to find out, so let's see how you can tell.

SMOOTH AS WATER

As we said before, ch'i moves in much the same way as water does. It likes to flow smoothly. Any space that air or water could flow smoothly around is likely to have good feng shui. The two dangers are that it will move too fast or too slowly – and perhaps even stagnate altogether.

風
水

There is a very simple technique for assessing which way ch'i will flow when it enters a room or an area of the territory outdoors. Imagine you are chasing a mouse or a rat around the area and just resisting the temptation to catch it. (If this is too difficult, you can imagine a fresh mouse, if you find you've imagined eating the last one.)

WHICH WAY WILL THE MOUSE RUN?

If the mouse gets up a lot of speed, for example down a straight corridor, the ch'i will also be flowing too fast down here. If it gets stuck in a blind alley, or misses out a corner, the ch'i will also stagnate or miss out this area. The mouse will cut corners and run round obstacles in a curved line – it won't make sudden 90 degree turns. Ch'i behaves in the same way; it likes rounded corners and curves, and soft rather than hard surfaces.

Here are a few guidelines about the kind of things that encourage both mice and ch'i to speed up or slow down.

Things that make ch'i and mice flow too fast: anything

straight – corridors, hedges, paths, gutters; open doors facing each other giving a straight run through; straight runs of stairs with no bends in them; chairs or other furniture arranged in straight rows.

Things that make ch'i and mice flow too slowly, or stagnate: alcoves, empty corners, dark spaces under worksurfaces or shrubberies, spaces you can't get at, anywhere cluttered, dead ends in rooms or outside.

Now you've finished this exercise it's OK to imagine catching the mouse.

WHERE WILL THE BIRD FLY?

There's another stage in the process, because ch'i moves in three dimensions and at all levels, while mice tend to stay on the ground most of the time. So now imagine that a bird has flown into this part of your territory, and you are pursuing it. Hold off catching it until you have imagined it flying up and down and round. Repeat the exercise of seeing where the bird flies fast or slowly, and which areas it misses out altogether. Once again, the ch'i will flow the same way.

The next thing we will look at is how you can remedy these fast or slow areas to encourage the ch'i to flow smoothly and harmoniously throughout your territory.

You may now catch your imaginary bird. Enjoy.

THE EIGHT REMEDIES

Any area that has poor feng shui can be improved by using a remedy. These remedies are objects or features that you place in the affected area to encourage the ch'i to speed up or slow down.

Each remedy has a section of the compass where it is most at home, but they can all be used any-where that is appropriate. It can be hard for cats to organize the same range of options as humans do, so if your choice is limited, use whatever you can lay your paws on.

LIGHT

Light remedies work anywhere that you want to encourage ch'i to flow, but they are best in the south section of the territory. Use them to encourage ch'i into dead corners and rooms that don't get enough sunshine.

If you know how to operate a light switch, this skill will be useful for introducing light remedies. However, we don't recommend that you experiment with cord pull switches except under expert guidance. If you can't use the light switch, don't worry – there are other options. Anything bright and shiny – especially if it is mirrored – will help. You can roll marbles into the area in question, or carry other bright objects and secrete them there. You'll find that if you have a human who wears jewelry, the dressing table can be an excellent source of shiny objects.

You will also find that to light up any really dark corners, all you have to do is leave something smelly there (see smell remedies), and sooner or later someone will come along and shine a bright light there to locate the source of the smell.

SOUND

Sound encourages ch'i, and enlivens it. You can use it to bring the ch'i into a dead area. Sound remedies are particularly effective in the northwest area of your territory. There are plenty of ways of introducing sound into an area. Humans often use wind chimes as a sound remedy, but cats tend to find them rather tangly. Out of doors, the squeaking of frightened small mammals does the trick nicely. Indoors, you may be lucky enough to find a cassette or CD player, or a radio, in the area in question. You just have to keep hitting all the buttons you can find until something happens.

One of the best techniques, inside or out, is to encourage your humans to produce the sound themselves. Something as simple as leaving a few entrails lying around

usually generates a few shrieks. Outside, you can create the same effect by digging up newly planted seed beds or young plants, or by using the children's sand box as a litter tray.

SMELL

Ch'i is enticed by smells, so if you want to encourage it into a corner or a dead area, you can urinate there. If you need strong encouragement you should spray, if you are able to. Another way to tempt ch'i into areas such as the cramped (but often important) spaces behind kitchen appliances or under furniture is to leave a dead mouse there. Or arrange to have your litter tray moved to the area where you need to apply the remedy (you'll find tips on how to do this later on). Smell remedies are particularly useful in the northeast of your territory.

LIFE

This remedy is best in the southeast section of your territory, to encourage ch'i in areas where it is stagnating. You can try bringing small mammals, birds, or other items of local fauna into the area. Bear in mind, however, that for the remedy to keep working they have to remain alive. They also have to remain in the area. One of the best creatures for achieving this effect is the common flea. They are less prone to wander off, and it's not difficult to leave them to live.

Plants also count as life remedies, but they must also be alive, of course. Grass will do, but if it has been half digested and then regurgitated it doesn't really count.

MOVEMENT

The life remedies involving animals rather than plants will work here, and so will anything else that moves. You could always keep moving yourself in this area but this can become tiresome when you've just eaten a large meal, the sun is shining, and everything is peaceful...

Far better to get something else to do the moving for you, so you can settle down to some not-moving-anywhere-for-a-bit. As well as using animals, try creating a breeze by opening a window (or arranging for it to be opened) and placing bits of string or paper where they will be blown around. You can also leave doors ajar so that they bang in the wind - this is a good sound remedy as well. Use movement remedies in the north.

STILLNESS

If the flow of ch'i is at all turbulent - for example in an area like a hallway that has lots of entrances and people milling around stirring the ch'i up – it needs to be calmed down using stillness, especially in the west of your territory. Any solid, stationary object will do for this purpose. How about something soft, curled up into a round shape, breathing gently, and emanating peacefulness? You'll come up with something if you think about it hard enough.

MECHANICAL DEVICES

You need to use a functional object here (these work best in the east) to encourage ch'i to be more active. A cat flap will do if you can arrange it in this part of the house. If you have one of those cat flaps that is operated by a magnet attached to your collar, find a way to discard the magnet – with or without the collar – in the appropriate place.

Failing that, a wristwatch is a good remedy. Next time one of your humans removes theirs, transfer it to a more useful place. This is in their own interest, since it is neither healthy nor necessary to be tied to time in the way that humans so like to be. You may have to conceal the watch in some way since your human might not recognize what a favor you're doing them.

STRAIGHT LINES

This remedy is ideal for encouraging ch'i to speed up, or for guiding it out of cluttered places, especially in the southwest. Find something long and straight, and place it in the problem area so that it points toward an area where the ch'i can flow more easily.

Good straight line remedies include straight twigs, whiskers, or household objects such as certain types of pasta. You will need to make sure that these items aren't inadvertently tidied away by your humans; it may be necessary to replace them from time to time.

FAME AND FORTUNE

The feng shui of this area influences your reputation with other cats. Are you regarded with disrespect and disdain? If so, don't worry – you can do something about it. First check to see if this area is missing completely – if so, there are three options. One is to place some reflective object facing the missing area, to bring it into the territory, visually at least. Most cats spend a good deal of time reflecting, so if you can't lay paws on a mirror, just sit facing the area and think.

The next option is to expand your territory into the fame area, other cats allowing. And the third is to reduce the size and shape of the rest of your territory so that the new, smaller shape has a fame and fortune area.

ATTRACTING THE OPPOSITE SEX

If you have a fame and fortune area, look at what remedies you can apply. If the area is quiet and sleepy, this may mean that you have little success with the opposite sex. You need plenty of noise (loud yowling or hissing types of noise are particularly good – the sort the radio makes if it isn't tuned properly). Then you need some nice smell remedies – spray around the room generously. And bring in some small animals to provide a life remedy. If this doesn't attract the opposite sex, nothing will.

If your problem is that you are too far down the pecking order with the neighboring cats, you will need to create a sense of strength in this area. You need plenty of calm here, to suit the sort of cat who stands its ground, so opt for stillness or mechanical devices. Clocks and watches are good since they contain coiled springs – a quality you need to emulate.

HEALTH AND HAPPINESS

Use the pah kwa to identify which area of your territory influences your health and happiness. Then consider whether these could be improved. If so, look for areas where the ch'i could flow better.

Maybe you have a vague feeling that you could be happier but you're not sure how to achieve it. The chances are that you'll find there are corners of the room that are not filled with ch'i; do something to remedy this.

Some things can lead to serious health problems. One cat we know lost her tail in an unpleasant accident. It turned out that her health and happiness area contained a chaise longue – nothing but a sofa with a piece missing from the back support section. If you have an unlucky object like this in the area, have it removed. Render it so useless that your human decides to throw it away.

USING MEDITATION

If your health and happiness area is missing altogether, it is probable that you are prone to lots of depressing visits to the v**. In this case, apply the techniques already mentioned to restore the area. The visits will become less frequent but – if they don't stop completely – you'll need to take further steps. Apply stillness remedies, if necessary using yourself: next time your human tries to pick you up to take you to the v**, apply extreme intertia to root yourself to the spot. You can reinforce the feng shui with another Chinese art: meditation. Think yourself too heavy to lift and, if you concentrate hard enough, your human will be convinced as well and be forced to abandon the project.

PLEASURE AND INDULGENCE

This is a particularly important area, and one that you should pay close attention to. Most of your best activities should happen here: eating and sleeping in particular. If this area is absent you are in big trouble. Do something about it at once.

This is the area to look at if your meals are not large enough or not frequent enough, if you can't find enough comfortable places to sleep, if you aren't allowed in the bedroom at night, if the curtains aren't drawn early enough in the morning on sunny days, if you are ever shut out of the house, are ever too cold, or if anything else ever happens to you that inhibits your pleasure in any way.

Make sure that the ch'i can reach every corner of this area, using light remedies. Leave no cranny unlit, or some desire will be unsatisfied. If you are deprived in terms of comfort – cushions, beds, and so on – use stillness or mechanical remedies on the most comfortable places to sit. If necessary, hide these remedies under pieces of furniture.

If your human's idea of a feeding regime is less than generous, use straight line remedies placed in brightly lit areas where the ch'i can move freely. Point them in the direction of your feeding area.

OPENING EVERYTHING IN SIGHT

If you are unlucky enough to be shut out of the house at night, or simply at times during the day, go around this area and open everything possible. If it's indoors, open cupboards, cans, doors, anything (although we don't suggest you attempt jam jars). If it's outside, open up passages through under-growth, sheds, clogged up holes in trees, and whatever else you can find.

NEW BEGINNINGS

orget this. It's all about change and unpleasant stuff like that, which is disruptive to sleep. Try to abandon this part of your territory, and make sure nothing new ever happens; ideally you want this section to be missing altogether.

If your life is full of unpleasant changes (forgive the tautology), this is the area to address to prevent any more disruption. It is possible that this is the area where your human likes to feed you, or keeps your litter tray. If this is the case, use the techniques later on in this book to have these things moved at once.

STAGNATING THE CH'I

If you cannot conveniently give up this part of your territory altogether, the next best thing you can do is to

encourage the ch'i to stagnate completely. Don't allow any light or sound into the area, keep all movement away from it as far as possible, and fill it with as many stillness remedies (other than yourself) as you can muster. Remove or disable any mechanical objects; you can stop most electrical equipment from working by applying fluid of some kind to the controls (avoiding the electrical cord) – no doubt you can find a way to do this.

Then back out slowly, and don't return to this part of your territory again. If there is any whisper of changes afoot, you will have to return to see if your remedies have been disrupted so that the ch'i has started flowing again. If so, replace them: you have to stop that ch'i from moving.

RELATIONSHIPS

The relationships section of your territory affects your relationships with both humans and other cats. If the ch'i in this area is disrupted and turbulent – for example, if the area is busy and cluttered, or has lots of entrances and exits – your relationships are likely to be turbulent or even aggressive.

In the case of neighboring cats this could be entertaining if you are bigger than them, or it could be unpleasant if the reverse is the case. In the case of humans it could mean that they are intolerant of such natural

風水

feline habits as bringing home little presents, or taking time to decide which side of a door to be on when the human is holding it open. You will need to introduce a calming remedy to the area to slow down the ch'i.

BETTER BONDING

If the ch'i is too sleepy and stagnating, you are likely to find that your humans don't bond with you as well as they might. Other cats who are not related to you, but share your territory, will have their relationships area in the same place, of course. All of you may find that you are distant and unaffectionate toward each other. Liven up the ch'i with a suitable remedy.

If this area is missing altogether, you probably live with someone who is away a lot. Use the techniques suggested earlier to remedy this. It may also help if you "lose" their passport and start sleeping in their suitcase; they should get the point.

KITTENS AND FAMILY

f you don't already have kittens, the first question to ask yourself is, do you actually want them? Kittens are delightful but they are also a handful, and they can grow up to be quite spitty with sharp claws and a shortage of respect for their elders.

Humans have a very unpleasant way of making sure that you don't have kittens. We won't go into details but it involves the v** and is quite unnecessarily cruel. It is far simpler just to eliminate this section of territory. Hand it over to a neighboring cat.

On the other paw, you might want kittens. If if this is the case (and if you haven't been thwarted by your human), you need to make sure that this area exists, and that the ch'i can flow freely throughout it. If the ch'i is disrupted you may find that the

pregnancy is uncomfortable (if you are female), or even that you don't know who the father is. If the ch'i stagnates, labor will be protracted and painful. The more cluttered the area, the more kittens there will be in the litter.

CREATING CALM

Once the litter arrives, things will be rather hectic. It will be extremely important to create as much stillness as possible in your kittens and family area.

If you are the father, go and sleep in this area, especially if it is well away from the area where the kittens are. If you are the mother, however, try to keep your kittens in this part of your territory, and encourage nurturing ch'i from the north.

Sleep as high up as possible in this area, to reinforce your position as top cat.

WISDOM AND EXPERIENCE

We have never met a cat yet whose territory had this area missing. Presumably this is because even without understanding feng shui, a cat would instinctively find it impossible to settle in such a place and would move on.

However, there can be problems resulting from a poor flow of ch'i in this area. One of the most common is poor concentration due to a tendency to fall asleep in the middle of thoughts. This is especially common when the wisdom area is in the north, the direction of the sleepy black tortoise. Some cats aren't bothered by this, mind you. But if you are, introduce noise and movement remedies to help you stay awake while you think.

CATZHEIMER'S DISEASE

Poor memory is another affliction resulting from stagnating ch'i in this area. This can manifest itself in such ways as forgetting that you have just eaten and constantly requesting more food, forgetting where the cat flap is and having to ask to be let in and out, and forgetting that you aren't allowed in the bedroom at night and sitting outside it meowing all night. These activities are not in themselves a problem, but where the cause is genuine amnesia this is obviously a worry. After all, the next stage can be catzheimer's disease, where you forget to eat altogether. It's crucial that you keep the ch'i moving: with straight line remedies, life, mechanical devices, smell, light and sound. Anything rather than forget to eat.

MATERIAL WEALTH

your wealth area determines how reassuring your stockpile of food is, how many toys and distractions you have, and so on. It also affects how many of your possessions your humans accept as being yours, and how many they misguidedly think they have rights over. If you're not sure about this, try moving things and seeing whether your human replaces them.

If you need further evidence, try the "chuckup test." Be sick on things. If your human accepts that the object is yours, it is for you to decide whether to clean it up or not.

If, however, they take it away and clean it up, they are obviously under the illusion that it belongs to them. In this case, you will need to improve the feng shui in your wealth area with light and life remedies.

One of the most persistent problems encountered by cats is having plenty of food supplied but of the wrong variety. As you know, there are cans of food... and then there are cans of food. What do you do if your human is stupid enough to supply the wrong cans?

REARRANGING THE FURNITURE

Look to your wealth area. You will find that the pointless objects that humans so like to clutter their houses with are arranged wrongly. They need rearranging. This may result in a change to another wrong variety of food. If so, try again. If a few items get broken this won't matter – it may even help. The important thing is to keep going until you find the arrangement that generates the food you need.

GETTING WHAT YOU
NEED FROM YOUR HUMANS

Y ou will have seen that there are certain alterations you need to make to improve the feng shui of your territory that will require cooperation from your human. Fortunately, this doesn't require them to understand the complex subject of feng shui; they don't need to know what they are doing, so long as they just do it.

The question is: how do you get them to make the changes that you can't manage? This is not as difficult as you might think, and this section is full of techniques for using humans to get what you need. The most important thing is to stand your ground. Remember the maxim: it doesn't matter how persistent they are, you can always be more persistent.

GETTING THE LITTER TRAY MOVED

Let's start with the simplest of all. If you have a litter tray you may

need it moved to a more suitable area, such as out of your wealth area and into the health section of your territory. Why should your human decide where your litter tray is kept? Their attitude is that they place the tray where they want it, and you deposit the output in it. But it makes far more sense for you to deposit the output where you want to, and pretty soon you'll find that they will move the litter tray to a position underneath where it comes out.

GETTING THE FEEDING AREA MOVED

This requires a similar approach. Refuse to eat from your bowl until it is moved. At mealtimes, stand where you would like the bowl to be kept. You could take the occasional chunk of food and drag it to your preferred spot before eating it. Remember to supplement this self-imposed fast with copious meals of the pick-your-own variety. If this doesn't work (and without reinforcement it may not), meow piteously. The next stage (if you need it) is to appear to be losing weight. Suck your cheeks in and even start to limp subtly when your human is around. Continue to stand in the new feeding place at mealtimes looking hopeful. It's only a matter of time.

GETTING FURNITURE MOVED

This is a little bit tougher, but it can be done. Treat the furniture in a way that humans don't like when it is in the wrong place, but stop once it is where you want it. If they move it back, start up again. Things humans don't like you doing to furniture include sharpening your claws on it, spraying on it, using it as a litter tray, and depositing unwanted entrails on it. If your human tries to respond by shutting you out of the area, refer to the next technique.

風水

GAINING ACCESS TO ALL PARTS OF THE TERRITORY

It can be crucially important to have access to certain parts of your territory, such as your pleasure and indulgence area. This can be easily achieved by making the human realize that shutting you out is more frustrating than letting you in. Do this by scratching at doors incessantly, or even meowing loudly if necessary. Persistence really pays off. You need to realize what your human is thinking, namely, "If I ignore this for long enough, eventually the cat will give up." Wrong – because you must think: "If I keep this up for long enough, eventually the human will give in." And they will.

GETTING CLUTTER REMOVED

This is fairly straightforward. You can keep knocking clutter off shelves and tables until your human removes it for you. Sometimes it may be necessary to break it before they will remove it. A few treasured

items will have to be smashed. If the human is around when you do this it is important to appear to be doing it by accident – even though we realize you will have to swallow your pride to allow yourself to appear ungainly.

GETTING THE HEATING TURNED UP

Warmth is obviously vital for ch'i to flow smoothly. Can you operate effectively without plenty of warmth? Of course you can't. And if you can't do it, how can

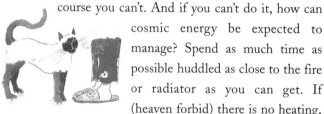

cosmic energy be expected to manage? Spend as much time as possible huddled as close to the fire or radiator as you can get. If (heaven forbid) there is no heating,

snuggle down inside the bed. The next stage – should you need it – is to shiver whenever the human is in sight, and look miserable. If this doesn't do the trick, start sneezing.

MAXIMIZING SUNLIGHT LEVELS INDOORS

When you need a light remedy in a section of your territory, this means that curtains or blinds must be

opened at first light — or
not closed the night
before. Once this has been
done, you will need to spend
some time sitting in any patches
of sunlight created to make sure that
they are suitable. Only by being
comfortable and relaxed in the sunshine
yourself can you be sure that the ch'i
will feel the same.

The standard technique here is to jump onto the
windowsill as soon as the sun rises. It's hardly your fault if
you knock any ornaments off because there is a curtain or
a blind in the way to prevent you from seeing where you're
landing. Your human will soon realize that their best bet
is to leave the curtains open so that you can see what
you're doing. If there are no ornaments, you will have to
use the alternative approach of climbing up the curtains
(your claws may get caught and damage the fabric — ah
well, it can't be helped). You can use this technique for
blinds or shutters (that sadly may get scratched or

風水

damaged). Again, your human will realize the sense of keeping these furnishings out of your way. By the way, do be careful with blinds - it is possible to get wrapped up in them if they roll up suddenly. Even if this isn't painful it is virtually guaranteed to be undignified.

These techniques should give you all the guidance you need to make sure that you can practice good feng shui throughout your territory. Remember: there is no point having humans if you can't make good use of them, and with good feng shui you should find that your relationship with them flourishes.

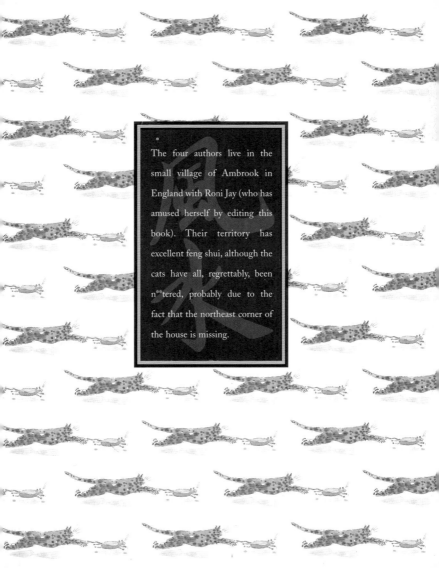

The four authors live in the small village of Ambrook in England with Roni Jay (who has amused herself by editing this book). Their territory has excellent feng shui, although the cats have all, regrettably, been n**tered, probably due to the fact that the northeast corner of the house is missing.

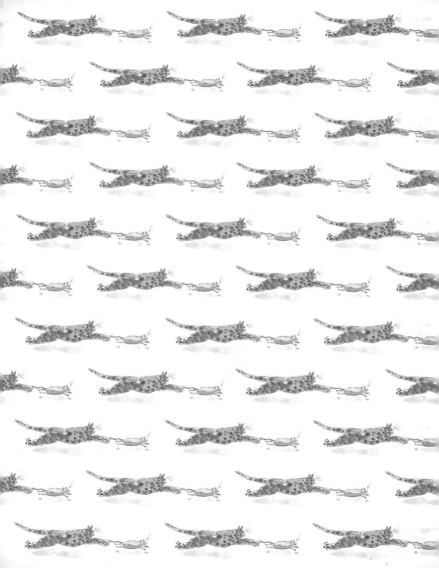